MY KENTUCKY
Poems of Earth & Home
Jimmie Ray Pennington

Copyright©Jimmie Ray Pennington, 2018
Cover Art Copyright©Kimberly Stalker, 2018
All Rights Reserved.
Printed in the United States of America.

Published by Agreement with Summerfield Publishing
New Plains Press
216 South 8th Street
Opelika, AL, 36801
newplainspress.com

Library of Congress Control Number
2018964979

ISBN 13: 978-0-9986857-6-2

Jimmie Ray Pennington 1952–
My Kentucky: Poems of Earth & Home
American Poetry, Kentucky Poetry, Nature Poetry, Mountain Poetry

No part of this book may be reproduced or transmitted in any form or by any means, electronic or mechanical, including photocopying, recording, or by an information storage and retrieval system (except by a reviewer who may quote brief passages in a review to be published in a magazine, newspaper, or on the Internet) without permission in writing from the artist(s) and publisher(s).

My Kentucky

Poems of Earth & Home

For every person there is a place which is held close to the heart, where a revisited memory can ease the pain of an entire lifetime. For me, this retreat of the heart is among the hills and hollows of my home. Kentucky, land of feuds and romance, of thoroughbreds and moonshine, bluegrass and soft ballads, deep dark mines and hardy souls, gentle flowing streams and towering cliffs, and a culture which reigns proud in its creation.

Jimmie Ray Pennington

For
Cayden
Jayden
&
Haleigh

Rustic Appalachia rises
to kiss a cockcrow sun
and bluegrass caresses
twilight when day is done.

From "This Kentucky"

TABLE OF CONTENTS

MY KENTUCKY 15
THE HOME PLACE BARN 17
AUTUMN WHISPER 18
SPRING RAINS 19
POEM FOR PAINT CREEK 20
OF HOME 22
WINTER SKY 25
TO STONE AND STREAM 26
ODE TO SUMMER'S CHILD 27
MAY TWILIGHT 29
EARTH HOME 30
PEACE 31
PLACES 32
THE TOBACCO BED 33
MOUNTAIN HOME PLACE 34
WINTER NIGHTS OF YESTERYEAR 35
MY APPALACHIA 36
CLOSE TO.... 37
SHADY HOLLER 38
SUMMER'S SILENCE 39
SILENCE 40
ODE TO THE RESERVOIR 41
SASSAFRAS AND SUMMERTIME 42
NATURE'S SYMPHONY 43
THE CROW 44
NIGHT 45
KENTUCKY EVENINGS 46
DINNER ON THE GROUND 47
OF EARTH AND HOME 48
SUMMER EVE 49
SPRING AWAKENING 50
TO APPALACHIA 51
THIS KENTUCKY 52
NOVA 53
ODE TO APPALACHIA 55
ODE TO BILLY RAY 57
VOICES OF OUR TIMES 58

SISTER APRIL 59
TO SONNET STREAM 60
THE PATH HOME 61
MOUNTAIN WOMAN 62
THE NIGHT WIND IS BLOWING 63
THE GENTLE THINGS 64
INTO WINTER 65
POEM AT DAWN 66
REFLECTIONS OF CHILDHOOD 67
BOURBON, BITTERS, AND BURLEY 69
EPITAPH 71
ACKNOWLEDGEMENTS 73
EPILOGUE [PLACES OF YOUTH] 75

15.

MY KENTUCKY

Near to Heaven, where
The rolling hills touch the night fall sky
I pause in somber thought
While whip-poor-wills sing
Their lonely songs which echo
Through misty hollers, and
I think of a long lost day
When Granpa would rise to say,
"The herbs in the hills
Wait for us, come now."
Money needed
Crops to be seeded
Precious commodities of nature's toil
Thriving deep within dark soil.
Blood root and sassafras bark buried deep,
Rich and dark, yellow root and may apple root
Treasures of our Appalachian home.
Memories of days
Come and gone
Where pocket money
Jingled in cut off jeans, and
The worries were so few–
Slippery Elm stripped of bark
Weighted burlap on my shoulder
Heading home at edge of dark,
Our pockets bulging with ginseng,
Knowing the cash it would bring
Would tide us over well into Spring.
Grandpa would pray for good season, and if not
He knew the reason,
And he knew we would make do
Because that's what you do
When Appalachia holds you nigh
Beneath her crisp blue skies.

16.

My days of youth, filled with peace,
Honesty and truth, and tradition taught well
By a Grandpa who had so much to tell.
If there were hardships I had to bear,
They were made much easier
Simply by his being there.
And now–memories
Are all I can hold close to my heart
And I will always treasure
Those days when we were never apart.

17.

THE HOME PLACE BARN
Weathered, weary gray when first we came,
victims of time; stress strained;
canted bow, slightly fro.
Slender poplar sentinels
tattooed with hearts of unknown lovers lost
burdened by weighted years,
those weary tiers.
Armored of regal oak now old knight,
still peeking 'neath rusty helmet of friendly tin,
even then.
Within hallowed hall
powdery carpet stirred remnants of decades
spent in faithful duty attended, and
scars, never mended.
Sagging hinged arms opened wide,
welcoming shelter from lazy summer storms;
in rhythmic tin–caught pelts
slumber melts.
Age old, worn by time
like home place, now gone,
cherished old friend
of youthful, peaceful day, collapsed.

18.

Autumn Whispers

Autumn whispers summer passing,
gentle days, children laughing,
frost swirling from old barn roofs
kissed by smiling sun.
Autumn whispers
leaves dancing on a gentle breeze,
hearts prancing
young loves–and old, and
hills painted in crimson and gold.
Autumn whispers, cozy talks
flickering hearths, unhurried walks
of crisp blue skies, and
new beginnings, the miracle of life.

19.

Spring Rains

Spring rains
Fall about me, like
Darkness falls
About the sun,
Slowly–softly.
Their gentle rhythm
On old tin roofs
Play soft ballads
Which touch my soul
And lends to sleep
A peaceful glow.

20.

Poem for Paint Creek (March 1974)
In wind swept days of March
I walked through golden fields,
And roamed o'er these peaceful hills–
I conquered towering cliffs
Climbing to their summit
To kiss the sky
Among the tree tops
There I have thought
With the silence of Nature around me
And I was overcome
By her many wonders–
I have drifted silently
With the gentle flow
Of this winding stream
Where sun-sparkled diamonds
Lie sprinkled on rippling waters
I have touched–no, embraced
The beauty of this land–
It has been my friend, and
I have come here often
To seek its freedom
Seek its wisdom–
I have found both
For hours on end, and
I have silently sat
Touching distant dreams
That lie hidden beyond
Blue-capped hills–
I have walked o'er
Pastures that edge
This majestic stream

21.

And felt the spirit
Of forefathers past
The labors of hours spent
Clearing this precious land
Here–their earthly home
And peaceful reward of life
And now in fertile soils
Have found Eternal Rest

Of Home

The simple want of simple days
often carries me back
to times of youthful memories
of family near; of mountain life, of home.
To the warmth of an old wood cook stove
in a crowded kitchen filled with love
and hot biscuits and gravy piled high
on an old china plate
from a matching and treasured set
collected over time from flour sacks
bought at a little country store.
Friends and neighbors
stopped in the evening to visit
and share the news, of things
like being in town at the five and dime,
or the call of heavenly Sunday meetings,
with families gathered,
oh how the way the rafters echoed
"Sweet By And By"
from gentle souls of grace and belief
of having found religion, baptized in a creek
where heart and soul are born again–
the sermon echoing on the breeze.
Precious memories of my land
Where life was simple
and love was free.
Where hope for a new season
would yield prosperous year and bountiful crop
from the age old fertile fields.
Root cellar, lined with mason jars,
Filled with food to tie us through
Winter season traditions with means and reason.

23.

A smoke house with salt-cured hams hung high,
with jams and jellies created from the vine,
the sweet rewards of life well spent
among ancient hills and hollows of home.
Fond reflections of culture old and true
carried through generations of life.
Recollected words of misty ballads
floating through backwoods
loaned to us mortal souls for a while.
I often walk among this land of home
where the flow of gentle streams cut through
towering sandstone
chiseled by the flow of time.
My mind dancing to the water's gentle rifts
as tall and slender poplars
planted firm and working hard, silently
stand their guard
over sandy, grassy banks
where mountain laurel weeps in the shade,
as the water trickles lazily on its way–
A life shared with kinfolks
by deep pools of cool water
easing the tanned and suffered skin,
after a day's hard labor
among steep hills that rise and fall
into a crisp clear blue sky.
The echoed stories of misty days, and
moonshine and stills hidden mystically in the pines
telling words of wisdom in story and rhyme,
written by the departed souls of yesteryear
passed down through generations
these found accounts of home.
All of these treasures held close to the heart
by those who have come and gone
and by those of us yet to part.

24.

My time upon this earth
shall come to end
and youth, I see, will carry on
to learn the beauty of this humble land,
and I pray they will cherish
the beauty and the heritage of home.

25.

WINTER SKY
sometimes i sit on the edge
of the world, and watch
the winter sky unfold beyond my reaching eyes,
and the cold gray of evening skies
swallow the mists of sun's last report–
orange, yellow, and now silver
veil until all light has failed,
and where blue sky once reigned
now glimmers not a single ray
of passing day
beyond thick and gathering clouds–
i speak
my thoughts aloud–(take me, too)

26.

TO STONE AND STREAM
This invading spring day
I sit on rocks of ages
thumbing through pages
of life's rewards–savoring her accords.
The mystic breath
of new born seasons speak in soft whispers
of westward breeze,
and hearts meld at ease.
Guardian willows bow stately and low
to majestic stream,
and the mind drifts
in tranquil dream.
The royal voice of water's course
echoes off towering cliffs
in rhythmic rifts.
Upon ancient stone I marvel–alone,
and of modest nature
there's her grandeur.

ODE TO SUMMER CHILD
Worn denim tucked and rolled
To mid-calf cuffs, but
Never quite secure 'nough
To stay suspended there (Who cares?)
Tanned by gentle summer day.
No school! Just endless play!
Cool mud and fleeting minnows
Await to tickle wiggly toes,
And steal youthful thought away.
Slate rocks flipped and tossed
Splutter, flitter, and glide
Reveling watery homes
Where crawdad and hog molly hide.
Awkward walks on slippery stones
Down creeks trickling too slowly,
No more than wasted time to show me.
Muscadine vine dangles to and fro
Under canopy of beech and oak–slices of summer breeze,
Childhood soarings, forever free.
The echoing calls of supper rings
through peaceful hills, and long afternoons surrender
To the call of whip-poor-wills.
With the younguns fed
And still a while till bed,
the porch swings creak and sway, as
hymns ride the evening breeze away–
serenading the passing day.
In dew-swept yards
lightning bugs display
from their glassy prisons,
as laughter mingles still
the calls of a shadowy hill.

28.

In feather-tick beds
youthful slumber sinks
into peaceful dreams
of adventures not yet seen.
On the edge of moonlit night
tomorrow gently smiles,
Awaiting Summer child.

29.

MAY TWILIGHT

Sitting, I attend to a softness from a May eve,
where playful breeze whispers between
the sleepy trees.
Twilight fills ensuing night,
as blue-gray skies
settle nigh, blanketing drowsy day.
In the calm of twilight's touch,
and nature's hush,
I gently merge with the peace of God's Earth.

30.

Earth Home

I have tried to touch rainbows,
filling fresh cleansed summer skies–
I have climbed to the top
of their brilliant arch
only to fall silently to earth,
and not a falling drop of rain
seeking out the warm
near moistness of soil,
I buried my face within its crust
to remain softly hidden in its cradle
sheltered from coldness
of winter's deadly touch, and
the loneliness
which I fear so much,
but fear need not be,
for my earth by God
holds me now in its loving arms
and here I shall sleep till eternity begin–
oh, peaceful peaceful rest.

31.

Peace

In whispers of the dancing wind
where earth and sky begin
to touch the tenderness of waking day
I pray peace.

32.

Places
There are places in our lives
close to the heart–
those which feel
safe and free of harm.
Places like a cherished farm
which seems to bring peace of mind,
and grows memories
through passing time.

33.

THE TOBACCO BED

I often recall piles of brush on narrow strips of Earth.
Dancing fire
and ashes gleaming into early evening.
Sparks riding high into the crisp, spring sky,
tobacco bed aglow
seeds wanting to grow.
A family toils
preparing endemic soils,
this, the Kentucky I know.

34.

MOUNTAIN HOME PLACE

Resting 'neath the east Kentucky skies of blue,
where rustic past blends with new.
Mountain home place embraces gentle hills drawing nigh,
memories of those days gone by.
The hillside pastures rebound with laughter of those far and near,
revisiting yesteryear.
From a church: ages old the treasured hymns
of yesterday still echo,
on a peaceful wind.
Heritage: again reborn by days of yore,
adorned where tradition entwines,
through a glimpse of time.
The home place
lends nostalgic blends
of early mountain days, of the people,
and of their ways.

35.

WINTER NIGHTS OF YESTERYEAR

Pleasant are the days of youthful past,
the memories of yesteryear.
Those which filled the heart with simple pleasures,
with heartfelt treasures.
At times, in the far reaches of my mind
I can smell potatoes roasting in the ashes of the hearth,
as children nod upon mothers' laps at the edge of dark.
The warmth of winter sleep tucked 'neath double wedding-ring,
and swallowed in tufts of feather ticks,
where dreams of licorice and peppermint sticks
dance in the land of nod.
The comfort of a winter moon hangs low in the Kentucky sky
painting hills and hollows with veil of silver glow.
The chill of wind that whistled through the pines,
memories etched in time.
The call of a lone hoot owl,
who lent a peace to winter sleep somehow, and
the rhythm of a crackling fire,
and its shadows dancing on papered walls.
Winter nights of yesteryear, forgotten pages
written through the ages
of youth and dreams,
where it was the simple things,
and it still seems it gave to life
the harmony of love and home.

My Appalachia

Among these majestic hills is a simple life of simple frills
and freedom of peaceful days where heritage thrives.
It is here I plant my being
deep within the heart of home
where tradition lends of itself
here in this commonwealth,
here in my Appalachia,
which cradles me nigh
and echoes those days gone by.
Where the treasured hymns of my Father's Father
still fill the Sunday breeze
from churches ages old,
those built upon foundations of faith
so very long ago.
Here beneath crisp blue skies, mountain ballads
caress a carefree life
and the call of whip-poor-wills
fill the warm summer night.
Where memories of youth resound
Where peaceful carefree days, unbound
My Appalachia, where farms cleared by our forefathers toil,
yielded boundaries of dark and fertile soil.
It is here I am planted in my life,
here that I thrive,
and it is here in my ending,
in these fertile soils,
that I will find my eternal peace.

CLOSE TO ...
Close to the heart and near to Heaven
where rolling hills touch a nightfall sky,
I close my eyes
and drift through the ages of time
the forgotten pieces of life's rewards.
Close to the fullness
of life
where loves remembered
spark the embers
of youthful hearts
and memories birth smiles of forgotten faces
in those faint traces–
I once again treasure life's simple pleasures.
Close to you
on a dew-kissed night
I think of the many things I have done right
in love and in life

Shady Holler

Dusty little road between the hills
up the holler to Uncle Buell's.
Cousins waiting, Anticipating.
Younguns scamper all about,
"Tag! You're it!"
Quick, another game before day runs out!
But–Shady holler surrenders
to Kentucky moon,
and childhood is gone
much too soon.

39.

SUMMER'S SILENCE

There is a peace among these spreading hills,
a harmony of the ages blended in stages
of shape, of size,
of natural co-existence with eternity.
Here, in summer's silence,
with my eyes closed toward the Heavens,
I touch immortality.
I find peace
as no other place can offer,
with the simplicity of dirt,
rock, and tree, touching the soul,
and filling the heart with ease
forever more.

Silence

I have felt silence
Fall across lives
Like long night shadows
Smothering
Slowly–Searching–Seeking
Within the reaches of the mind.
I have watched as silence
Overcame the old
And they gave life away to death–
I have seen them reach out
For one last hold to life
Only to lose to death's stronger
Pull.
Speechless–their eyes
Reaching
For eternity somewhere beyond.
I have watched as silence
Crept in–slowly as a thief
To fill the musty rooms
Where life's last battles are fought.
I have known the silence
Which fills the hearts
Of the living who mourn death.
I have seen their silence spill
Into the tears of sorrow
Sorrow that lingers–echoes
Within hollow church halls.
And I have watched as the living
Wearily pushed silence away
To return to life.

41.

Ode to the Reservoir
misty eyes watched water rise
day by day flooding memories away
imprisoned in cells of watery swells
pastures green lost to peaceful dream.
heavy depths smother youthful
searching steps, and paths trod now lie buried,
lost in muddy sod
towering cliffs of ancient stone
surrender themselves and are quietly gone
timeless creation hides beneath recreation,
and earthen arms
hug and caress forefather's farms,
sacrificed to protect land and lives.

Sassafras and Summertime

The trees stood tall on ridge tops away,
and I as a child invaded summer day.
The breeze whispered softly upon lofty bows dancing,
where beneath young hearts trekked by prancing.
A crackling carpet of leaves rustling,
cushioned young feet lazily shuffling
on paths of yesterday's ware.
Eyes searching the benches and hollers there
with Papa for treasures of sassafras
and savory smell of spicy bark upon a summer day.
The black, cool soil
of nature's timeless toil
moist on bended knees under canopy of hardy trees.
Small, quick hands plunged into earth,
revealed hiding roots beneath the dirt,
deep where thick bark yields
until burlap bag was plumped and filled.
A spicy cup of fresh brewed tea
sipped under a familiar shade tree,
listening to stories of Papa's youth,
wondering is this fiction or truth?
The herbs and barks of my Kentucky home,
learned on journeys come and gone,
planted in my mind
like sassafras and summertime.

43.

NATURE'S SYMPHONY

In the stillness of the velvet night
when darkness shades the sense of sight
with eyes closed toward the sky
my ears hear a hidden life.
I marvel, as the hectic sounds of day
gives way to the silence of nature's cheery voice.
Where a symphony of creatures sing in chorus
from stages of shadowed shrubs
lit by the twinkles of dangling lightening bugs.
In the warmth of the breeze,
the midnight performance
is applauded by an audience of dancing trees,
and by me.

The Crow

Ebony grace, weightless in silver-blue sky.
Devil's discourse,
his lesser of evil, of course.
With perfect ease upon torrents of summer breeze,
acrobat of loops and dives,
curious he glides to the ground.
Head erect, with stealthy steps,
piercing eyes inspect the ground,
intent upon the possession of all he has found.

45.

NIGHT

Night, comes marching on the path of tomorrow,
greeting a timid sun.
The footfalls of darkness
weigh the brimmed smile, of a waning day.
Beyond the crested earth
tomorrow waits for a new awakening.

46.

KENTUCKY EVENINGS

Peaceful, those Kentucky evenings
as night begins to fall, slowly
on the hollers of home,
and the rain doves coo their soothing song.
When the melting sun paints the ridge tops,
with strokes of lucent glint,
a warm and golden tint.
In the still, the trees
seem to pause in the twinkle of that fading light,
awaiting the cool of coming night.
In the shadows of the hills
whip-poor-wills begin to cry,
as dusk sprinkles stars across a lucid summer sky.
In the calm, I ponder
as the Kentucky moon begins to softly glow on days of yonder,
those far away memories, which often warm my weary soul.

47.

DINNER ON THE GROUND
I remember Sundays
When hymns were lifted away
By waves in unison from paper fans
From benches all in a row,
Sending gentle waves to and fro.
The younguns whine, aroused
At the ring of the preacher's voice
Echoing off the distant hill,
Far beyond gathered crowds
Where the sermon lingers still.
Tables covered side by side
With checkered tablecloths
Summer and fried chicken blend
In hungry, youthful thoughts
And stomachs growl for meetin's end.
Here, hell has no fiery holds
For scripture rings out
Among the gathered souls,
And sweet song and joyful shout
Fills graveyard about.
Fathers and Mothers, gone
With yesterday's passing
Lie silently listening
'Neath the green grass of home
Nearer them–to home.
In prayer kneeled down
The sermon closed,
both Souls and plates overflow
When dinner's on the ground.

48.

OF EARTH AND HOME
Humbled by the majesty,
the mystics of this earth,
I stand upon the dust of our primordial birth.
With eyes which see,
and a heart that's meek
I touch the vastness,
the greatness of creation.
Here, upon narrow swath of Mother Earth,
I embrace the splendor of my cherished home.
This Kentucky, which still caresses the heritage of days
long since gone.
I surrender to these eastern hills
where kindred spirit
spills from hidden hollers.
This land of feuds, of romance, of
peaceful abundance, and earth enhanced.
Here I thrive,
I grow amidst stately child
of earth, amidst her freedom,
her generosity–her mirth.

49.

Summer Eve
far in the hollow
a whip-poor-will calls
summoning slumber
as night gently
falls

50.

SPRING AWAKENING

Night unfolds like a crimson rose,
kissed by the silver moon.
Caressed by whiff of twilight's touch,
gardens bloom
and night sings to Spring
awakening.

TO APPALACHIA

Saturday mornings begin at nine
on the corner by the five and dime.
The streets beginning to stir, and youthful mind's set awhirl.
The old men in their faded over-alls are planted,
as spiraled cedar falls from their sticks
whittled slowly, and weekly debates begin to freely flow.
The gentle hills are nestl'd nigh,
as sleepy town yawns 'neath waking sky.
Traditions of Appalachia reaches,
to those who listen, it teaches.
Through the eyes of age–enhanced,
the simplicity of life, romanced.
Within treasured, incessant lore,
lingers the cherished days of yore.
Borne of dignity,
we have transpired from the dreams of those
which sired the birth of home
in this fruitful land,
planted among hills and hollows we stand,
as did those fathers of present–past.
In timeless tradition taught steadfast,
we envision the rich and bountiful birth
of our youth among this Mother Earth.

This Kentucky

Ageless, this comely land born of troubled birth,
where eternal wonders poise on brim of rugged earth.
Etched by fret of time, this thoroughbred,
this Kentucky of mine.
Crested ridge tops away cloaked
by unbounded sky cradle farms and hollows
limning days gone by.
Those days of hardships
found in struggles
among a dark and bloody ground.
Rustic Appalachia rises to kiss a cockcrow sun
and bluegrass caresses twilight when day is done.
From width to breadth, gentle land of peace
ever giving of itself, this meadowland,
this peaceful commonwealth.

Nova

The love of my life–Marie
But to you she was just, Ree.
Did you know you were her strength in life?
Her guiding light
Through sorrow and strife.
For her, you were always there
With your pipe in hand
At rest in cane bottom chair.
At times, I thought that chair to be
Your earthly throne,
And in the kitchen by the old wood stove
Your place to be alone.
The image, still there within my mind,
Small of frame and callused by time.
A Granny to everyone,
Mother to a special few.
Though your composure, rough and hardy,
Your voice fell soft as the sweet morning dew.
I often recall the whimsical things you said,
"Now, Ree you got a good man, Aye Ned,
Treat him right and *he'll* take care of you, instead."
You were so special,
And your love for people so true.
You were at home there nestled between the hills,
Plain and simple with no frills.
With scarf bound about your graying mane,
And slacks to warm your petite frame.
Your Sunday meals
Were pleasures for my wife and son,
And they hated to leave when the day was done.
Sometimes I would visit, too,
But I knew–Sundays were for Ree, and you.
Your life was spent as a guiding light,

54.

And justly was your name "Nova,"
A star that burns brilliantly bright,
Then ceases to glow–
You taught the love of my life so well,
And the love for you within her heart,
My mere words could never tell.
May you rest for eternity by the throne of God,
And may he reward you well,
For the earthly burdened paths you trod.
And, for your darling Ree,
I promise to protect and love her dearly.

7/30/93
(At Peace)

55.

ODE TO APPALACHIA
Here the rustic hills of pastel green
are caressed by the bluest skies I've ever seen.
In that soft and aesthetic sky
meandering clouds float lazily by,
and I pause to savor the flavor of this land
the beauty, and the peace which it commands.
Appalachia cradles me in her arms
with the remnants of her many charms.
The idioms of her people ring in the hills
like the church bells of long ago, echoing still.
This land caresses me, possesses me,
and I cherish its freedom and serenity.
A simple life, with want of nothing more.
Heartfelt reflections of the days of yore,
where tireless labors and toils
struggled to amend endemic soils,
where many bounties flourished
and hardy souls were nourished.
Where the stately faces of mountain life
sung hymns which floated on the breeze at night
from porches perched above the fields.
Those lyrics of my kindred soul lingers still,
and with a humble heart I'm proud
to be heir to my forefather's decree.
My thoughts drift freely, often filled
with past voices, and their iron clad will.
Their words of wisdom often resound
the refinement of a culture renowned,
where strength and humbleness
intertwine in an existential realm, divine.
Built upon devotion and intensity
and molded from hope and simplicity,
a flowering culture centuries old

56.

forged from hardships untold
where necessity and opportunity birthed
my people's strength and unity.
Appalachia, ever stately and ever true,
there could be none grander than you.
My breath is drawn from your gentle winds
from your noble children, I descend,
to take my place among your fertile fields
and reap the virtues which you yield.

Ode To Billy Ray

You might have been a bit wild, it is true
much like the hills which spawned you
as free as the blowing winds
always close by a trusted friend
through the misfortunes and losses
and loves which came with a cost,
with hazel eyes that smiled behind
a rough and rowdy soul refined
steadfast in your stance and stature
always willing to embrace your nature
never regretting your simple life
never swaying from what was right
you were a man with the soul of a boy
always brimming with love and joy
facing your adversities head on,
unfaltering until your will was done
a free-spirited child of the Kentucky hills:
adventurer, cantankerous, never stilled,
you faced your life at your own speed,
never succumbing to lust or greed,
simply born and gently placed,
among fertile hills you were graced,
with an openness and an attitude
which reflected your gratitude,
you echoed the vibrant appeal
of your cherished and treasured hills,
and with a voice, soft
as the mountain breeze
humble enough to pray on bended knees
your devotion to life, family and friends,
carried you to a peaceful end.

58.

VOICES OF OUR TIMES
(Dedicated to the musicians of Country Music Highway U.S. 23)

There's a road that winds
Through gentle mountains,
Intertwined.
Here stars rise beyond
That winding road
To shine on discs
Of platinum and gold.
Here young voices
So sweetly sing
With hopes of touching
Distant dreams.
From Greenup to Letcher,
And the sleepy hollows
That lie between
Are the stars not yet seen.
Here the sound
Of soft ballads played
Linger within
Misty mountain days.
Singing stories of my home
In melodies of tender song.
Songs filled with memories
Of those we have lost
Those who live forever
Within our thoughts.
The roots of country
Are planted still
Here among
These fertile hills.
Through our music
And words of rhyme
Echo the voices
Of our times.

Sister April

The velvet touch of dawning
awakens slumbering hills
as the world stirs, yawning.
Stars smile from worlds away
while Sister April greets
another day.
Misty eyes peek o'er mounds of Appalachia,
silhouetted
against the newness found.
And the words of yesterday
lie silent, listening
to the song of the new day.
Sister April, who held me nigh
in my first glimpse of life
softly bids farewell to night.

60.

TO SONNET STREAM
Above, rises earthen dam of clay and rock.
Tamped by weight of steel
and man,
And there in captive,
held lake ends to stand.
Below, at feet of manly creation,
water speaks from tongues of rocks,
whispering soft words of rhapsody.
Each tumbling droplet,
a syllable of sonnet
seeking mate to unite,
and verse to write.
Mingled there in gentle stream,
the tears of love also flow.
They speak in babbling cries,
and sonnet listens,
understanding "Why"
Within their touch of pain and love,
sweet marriage of tears
and words dissolve into tomorrow.
Quenched by droplets of singing stream
they join a journey of evermore.
Tears of love and rock,
spoken word, seekers of peace
drift with melodic stream
lost to the call of poetic dream.
Searching for verse unheard,
united in today and the days of yore,
seeking the eternal shore
of Mistress Sea, and her infinity.

61.

THE PATH HOME

There's always a path which leads you home
sometimes its traveled all alone.
Sometimes its filled with laughter of friends
who share the journey to the end.
Sometimes the path is of memories known,
of youthful days retouched
when we have grown.
Sometimes it's filled with tears and pain
and lonely days of falling rain.
But no matter how the path is laid
there are memories
waiting to be made.
When life weighs heavy remember
you're not alone–
just follow the path
which leads you home.

62.

Mountain Woman

The sun rose over the mountain
To rouse me from my bed so soft,
And the thoughts of my woman's loving
Is still fresh on my mind.
It looks like it's going to be
Another beautiful day,
And together you and I
Will watch it all roll away.
Woman you fill my life
Like the sun fills the summer sky,
And loving you feels so right
I'm never going to say goodbye.
It seems I searched a lifetime
Looking for a love like yours–so warm,
And it's true I never found that love
Until I met you.
Mountain woman you bring me such joy
Mountain woman, tell me don't you know,
You've made a man of this country boy.

(9/30/77- To Marie)

63.

THE NIGHT WIND IS BLOWING

The night wind is blowing
Lonesome down the holler tonight
And the pale moon is glowing
With a soft blue light.
Sometimes as I sit here
Trying to chase away the pain
I swear I can hear
The wind whispering your name.
Oh–lonesome is the heart
That gives itself freely
Only to be torn apart
And hurt so very deeply.
The mountain mist seems to swirl
Through the lonesome pines
And the memory of your kiss, girl
Is heavy on this heart of mine.
I remember the promises you made
To always love me true
Why did you have to go away?
How I wondered what I had to do.
The wind is blowing
Lonesome down the holler tonight
And the moon is glowing
With its soft blue pallor of light.

The Gentle Things

The gentle things in life soothe the
soul. The calm of a spring eve, when
the peepers screech and croak from a
distant hiding.
When the cool breeze plays with new
born leaves; and robins serenade the
passing day. The freshness of first mown
grass announcing winter has passed
at last.
The playful laughter of young lovers
touched by Cupid's seductive arrow.
The gentle things in life are always
the best to know.
The peace of a young season's sun
melting behind the hills when the day
is done. The softness of a velvet
twilight; which falls like a peaceful sleep.
Lightening bugs which sparkle and
twinkle as if earthly stars; often
from prisons of Mason jars. Youthful
memories; precious possessions of days
of yore, seldom touched anymore. Now
hurried days of demanding steal
youth and memories away.

65.

INTO WINTER

Fall has begun to brush the leaves
with its palette of many colors
and I wait for the frost
to lie heavy on the early mornings
as Winter knocks on the door of tomorrow
and the cold wind is longing to howl.
I pause within the silence waiting for
the winter nights cold and chilled
The short days will be laden
by the Winter suns withdrawal
which silently stalls
the call of the seasons passing.
I know Winter will seem forever lasting
as the cushioning snow silences footfall
on the path as I scurry home.
Hanging my scarf, shaking off the cold
from my aged and weary bones
unchanging in my tone
I will mumble and complain
quietly cursing the pain.

66.

Poem At Dawn

I watched the dawn
as she opened
her sleepy eyes
wide—wider still.
I watched as she smiled
upon the gentle earth
her warm awakening.
I listened to the words
the wind was singing;
in my mind the melody
lingered soft and free.
I rolled with the waves
of open sea
to the blue horizon,
and touched distant lands
that lie beyond.
Give to me tomorrow;
and I shall live to touch
the wisdom of distant worlds
beyond endless skies.
I will touch the many
wonders of life unseen,
and smile at thought
of gentle dawn ...

67.

REFLECTIONS OF CHILDHOOD

The unrehearsed days of childhood
seemed to be endless
as streams of classes dragged by
and teachers sat before me
like stone-faced monarchs
upon their wooden thrones of wisdom.
But often I could drift
beyond the confines
of the stuffy room
like a paper boat set adrift
on the fountain of a Sunday-filled park
managing to conquer raging seas
to sail peaceful and tranquil waters
to new adventures.
Often I would escape through
glances out the window
and travel highways beyond my sight
searching for unknown wisdom
hidden somewhere in future.
And when the bell sounded
at three o'clock sharp
I could feel Summer
draw one day closer.
I would rush to the football field
and lie on my back in the cool grass
watching as my kite danced
on the Spring wind, wondering
if worlds could exist
beyond the blueness of the sky.

68.

Now the childhood teachers are gone
yet, I am still learning, and
the only difference now
experience is my teacher
and I still wonder how worlds exist
beyond the blue sky.
I am still traveling those highways
which lie beyond my sight
searching for the wisdom hidden there.

69.

BOURBON, BITTERS, AND BURLEY

Appalachian born and raised
of gentle nature and gently placed
among the hills and hollers
laboring hard to earn a dollar.
When I first came to know him
he was old; even then
rough and rugged
with a sly 'ole grin.
Rowdy and relentless
mean and ornery I guess,
his face edged by the labors of life.
He taught me wrong but also right,
taught me about bourbon whiskey
and the burn it could yield to the tongue
of one so gullible and young.
He told me I would do well
to leave it alone or I'd go to hell.
I learned of his life among the hills
of his commitment and free will.
He spoke of hardships he had known
during The Great Depression
and how he had overcome oppression.
Learned how bitters made and brewed
provided income to tide him through.
He sold his tincture for more
than a quart of moonshine would bring
and swore they could cure most anything.
I do regret that I never learned
the secret recipe of that brew–
I guess he was the only one who knew
all that made his concoction
so good, and I would like to go back
and ask him if only I could.

70.

I learned from him how to pile brush
and burn the ground to kill the weeds
and prepare a 'baccer bed for sowing seeds–
he taught me how to grow a burley 'baccer
crop to have whatever I should need.
I learned the language of the mountains
the stories of loss and those of gain
from a Grandpa tough as nails
yet gentled with age and sometimes frail.
I was glad to know, at the at age of seventy-eight
that it had not become too late for him
to find religion to save his weary soul–
I remember that was just a little while
before The Lord said,
"Ed, it's time for you to go."

Epitaph

i touched life.
life led me. i was blind
but could still see. i sought love
love evaded me.
i wrote, no one
read, so i died.

ACKNOWLEDGEMENTS
(SOME OF WHICH HAVE BEEN SLIGHTLY ALTERED FROM THE ORIGINALS)

"My Kentucky" *Kentucky Monthly Magazine*, 2017 Literary Edition. "The Home Place Barn" *Pegasus*
"Autumn Whispers" *Pegasus*
"Spring Rains" *Pegasus*
"Winter Sky" *Promise Magazine*
"Ode to Summer Child" *Kudzu*
"Mother Earth" *White Ash*
"Winter Nights of Yesteryear" *Pegasus*
"To Appalachia" *Kudzu*
"The Path Home" *Pegasus*
"Poem for Paint Creek" *The Dakota House*
"Dinner on the Ground" *Blue Ridge Traditions*
"Summer Eve" *The Crucible*

COVER PHOTOGRAPHY,
KIMBERLY STALKER

Kimberly Stalker is a licensed Physical Therapist Assistant, and photographer, from Kentucky. Her photos have won several awards in local and regional shows.

75.

PLACES OF MY YOUTH
AN EPILOGUE

I have dabbled with the idea of writing for a little over three decades now. At the tender age of ten, I reluctantly scribbled out my first story, and that for some now for- gotten teacher. The experience was actually an introduction to a distant and undiscovered love.

I was born in Ohio and relished the small town of my youth. My hopes at ten were to always be where I was, and as I was at that point in time. Those hopes were short lived, though.

When I turned twelve, failing health forced my father into early retirement. My family was uprooted and moved to the Appalachians of eastern Kentucky. I was transplanted from the busy, active explorations of my hometown into a completely different atmosphere. The loss of youthful friendships weighing heavily on my shoulders, so I tried to find ways to fill my days of that first friendless summer. In a rural area where kids of your own age lie scattered and hidden in secluded hollows, which lie tucked away beyond blue-capped hills, you soon learn to fill days any way you can. I chose to occupy that summer tagging after my Grand Pa, who had spent his life in Appalachia. He in turn (unknowingly) gave birth to my desire to write. I would often just sit and watch as he wiled away a summer day. With his feet propped against the porch post, and at rest in his cane-bottomed chair, he would whittle away the day. The scent of cedar slivers and the precisely aimed amber spurts of tobacco juice still linger in the mists of my mind.

Out of lack of kids to share my days (thank goodness) he became my teacher, not in a scholastic sense, but rather the teacher of my soul; my mentor. I followed him into the rugged terrain of my new found home, and learned things which books could never teach me. I listened to the stories of his distant youth with curiosity and awe. The hardships and the light-hearted days of his life blended into a melody of peaceful existence.

76.

Through his eyes, I was introduced to the wonders hidden within the hills. Together we shared long days gathering herbs, roots, and barks from the depths of cool hollows beneath a canopy of towering oaks, beech, poplar, and sassafras. I learned I could make pocket money from ginseng, bloodroot, and other valuable herbs. Those days of gathering not only filled my pockets with the jingle of coins, but flooded the journal of my mind with the stories of my tomorrow.

It was 1964 when I moved to Kentucky, and I became a student of my Grand Pa's wisdom. I guess I didn't understand then that I was being tutored in the ways of Appalachian life. I was glad he was there to distract my mind from the loss of my distanced friends. I began to write occasionally that summer. From time to time I would jot down a few simple lines about something I had seen or had done in the woods with Grand Pa. Ten years after my arrival to Kentucky, Grand Pa passed away. I lost a companion and a teacher, but the heritage of his life and his love of his home had been instilled deep into my soul.

Twenty-five years have passed, and now on cold winter days when time seems to linger, I gather together the words from the journal of my youth. I stare longingly at my keyboard, anxious for my fingers to walk into the past.

My thoughts have become intermingled in the treasured words of Grand Pa and in the beauty of my adopted home. The stories I remember hearing, beneath lush green canopies of towering trees on long summer days, are reborn. Time seems to melt into an endless journey when words flow freely from the past.

If I write and no one ever reads, I have not lost anything. Instead, I have regained a cherished part of my own being, and transcribed it to paper to be discovered someday by another. My only desire would be that I have been successful in carrying the person who reads my words to those treasured places of my youth.

(1998)

www.ingramcontent.com/pod-product-compliance
Lightning Source LLC
Chambersburg PA
CBHW060503110426
42738CB00055B/2597